Addiction: A Problem of
EPIDEMIC PROPORTIONS

Stephanie Lundquist-Arora

San Diego, CA

© 2021 ReferencePoint Press, Inc.
Printed in the United States

For more information, contact:
ReferencePoint Press, Inc.
PO Box 27779
San Diego, CA 92198
www.ReferencePointPress.com

LIBRARY OF CONGRESS CATALOGING-IN-PUBLICATION DATA

Names: Lundquist-Arora, Stephanie, author.
Title: Addiction : a problem of epidemic proportions / by Stephanie
  Lundquist-Arora.
Description: San Diego, CA : ReferencePoint Press, [2021] | Includes
  bibliographical references and index.
Identifiers: LCCN 2020011901 (print) | LCCN 2020011902 (ebook) | ISBN
  9781682829219 (library binding) | ISBN 9781682829226 (ebook)
Subjects: LCSH: Drug addiction--United States. | Drug abuse--United States.
  | Substance abuse--United States.
Classification: LCC HV5825 .L85 2021 (print) | LCC HV5825 (ebook) | DDC
  362.290973--dc23
LC record available at https://lccn.loc.gov/2020011901
LC ebook record available at https://lccn.loc.gov/2020011902

Contents

A Pervasive Problem

On September 25, 2019, an eleven-month-old baby nearly died from a heroin overdose in Chester County, Pennsylvania. As his heroin-using parents slept in the front seat of their car, the little boy sat alone in the backseat. While Kristen Bristow and Charles Salzman Jr. slept, their son found and ingested some of their drugs. The boy's grandfather called the police when he found the boy unresponsive in the backseat of the car. First responders administered three doses of Narcan, a drug used to revive people who are dying of opioid overdose. The baby survived. His parents were charged with aggravated assault, endangering the welfare of a child, and recklessly endangering another person. Assistant District Attorney Michael Noone says, "That child was overdosing before [his] first birthday because of the actions and addictions of the parents."[1]

This type of story is becoming more and more common as drug addiction pervades the United States. Americans aged eighteen to twenty-five are the most likely to use illegal drugs, which are highly addictive. According to the Addiction Center, a website that provides information about addiction and treatment, approximately 2.1 million Americans misuse opioids. Based on survey research, a 2018 report by the National Center for Health Statistics further estimates that 11.2 percent of people in the United States, twelve years and older, had recently used an illegal drug. This drug addiction not only ruins lives but also is costly to society.

Behavioral Addictions

Although not as common as substance addiction, which involves drugs and alcohol, behavioral addictions can also lead to troubling and sometimes tragic outcomes. People can develop addictions to gambling, social media, video games, food, shopping, sex, and the internet, among other things. Substance and behavioral addictions are not exactly the same, but there are similarities. With substance addictions, users experience short-term rewards (such as an immediate high or a brief sense of calm). They also develop powerful physical cravings and feel disturbed when they cannot get more of the substance. With behavioral addictions, people often experience an emotional high or euphoria similar to what occurs with substance addiction. And like substance addicts, people with behavioral addictions can become so caught up in the activity that they neglect everyone and everything else in their lives.

> "That child was overdosing before [his] first birthday because of the actions and addictions of the parents."[1]
>
> —Michael Noone, an assistant district attorney in Chester County, Pennsylvania

Melanie Tait has an addiction to food. In an article for *The Guardian*, she writes, "Food is the great love of my life. I've forsaken everything else for it. I've chosen it over lovers, over experiences, over family, over my career." She explains that her memories of places are all tied to food—not shared over conversation with friends and family at a dinner table, but most often consumed in her bedroom in secret. She associates high school with apple muffins, candy bars, and butter-and-cheese cracker sandwiches. Although she has stolen from her parents repeatedly and maxed out her own credit card on late-night fast-food binges, her mother and father do not believe that she has an addiction to food. She writes, "They think I'm weak. That I can't control myself. That I'm lazy."[2]

The ways in which addiction is understood are evolving. In the case of many behavioral addictions, society largely believed those afflicted had character disorders and should just demonstrate self-control. Some people continue to subscribe to this belief. They still contend that addiction results from a lack of willpower. Patrick Carnes is an internationally known authority and speaker on addiction and recovery issues and author of *Out of the Shadows*, a book defining sex addiction. Carnes writes, "Today we understand that addiction is an illness—a very serious disease. Furthermore, problems such as drug, food, gambling and sex addiction are actually related and rely on similar physical processes. Most important, we know that people can get help and that a good prognosis exists."[3]

Technology and New Addictions

Whereas some addictions have been around for a long time, other addictions have developed with technological advancements. Modern technologies have led to more productivity and the ability to communicate across great distances, but these advances have a social price. Prior to the introduction of the tablet in 2000, a toddler mesmerized by a colorful 10-inch (25 cm) flashing screen while being pushed in a cart through a grocery store would not have been a common scenario. Before video games, children and teens would not likely have spent hours indoors with joysticks or controllers and game consoles. Teens and adults alike did not have the compulsion to check their social media accounts multiple times an hour to make sure they were not missing anything. Before smartphones, people who got together for a meal or coffee were more likely have an uninterrupted conversation.

All of this has changed. The average smartphone owner unlocks his or her phone 150 times per day—over 9 times an hour. TechJury, a team of software experts, further reports that 66 percent of the population exhibits signs of nomophobia, or mobile phone addiction. Americans' cravings for the latest news, gossip,

As smartphones have exploded in popularity, many teens and adults feel compelled to repeatedly, sometimes obsessively, check their messages and social media accounts.

pictures, likes, reviews, and messages allow them to be more connected but, arguably, also more alone than they have ever been before. Experts say that their addiction to their screens is socially isolating.

Technology has even helped worsen old addictions. Gambling addicts no longer need to go to a casino; they simply log on to their computers. Sex addicts no longer need to spend time engaging in long conversations at a bar for a hookup; they just need to swipe one way or another on an app. The internet and smartphones provide all the information addicts seek, often to their detriment.

Addiction has become widespread. Steve Sussman, a professor of preventive medicine, psychology, and social work at the University of Southern California, suggests that about half of the

> "How we respond to this crisis is a moral test for America. Are we a nation willing to take on an epidemic that is causing great human suffering and economic loss? Are we able to live up to that most fundamental obligation we have as human beings: to care for one another?"[4]
>
> —Vivek Murthy, the nineteenth US surgeon general

US population suffers from at least one addiction—and sometimes more. More than likely, those not afflicted by addiction have a family member or close friend who is addicted. Addiction in the United States is a pandemic. It is taking lives, ruining health, and destroying families. Opioid addiction, in particular, is wreaking havoc. While serving as the US surgeon general, Vivek Murthy issued a report about America's opioid addiction crisis. His words can be applied to the broad scope of addiction in contemporary life. He wrote, "How we respond to this crisis is a moral test for America. Are we a nation willing to take on an epidemic that is causing great human suffering and economic loss? Are we able to live up to that most fundamental obligation we have as human beings: to care for one another?"[4]

Chapter One

What Is Addiction?

Addiction is an overwhelming desire (or an irresistible, persistent impulse) to engage in a particular activity or use a specific substance despite its destructive effects. Not doing these things can make the addicted person anxious or sick, and usually that person is unable to stop without help. Addiction does not have just one face. It does not have a particular age, gender, or race, and it afflicts people from all socioeconomic backgrounds.

Education and money do not protect a person from developing an addiction. Even people trained in the workings of the mind and body—who use that knowledge to care for others—can fall prey to addiction. In 2018, an anonymous medical doctor shared his addiction story with Physician Health Services, a nonprofit corporation that provides confidential consultations to physicians. The doctor described himself as having a thriving medical practice and a loving family. But this successful exterior belied the troubles within. He began taking stimulants to stay awake and study for exams while in medical school. After graduation, he found the demands of his practice overwhelming and began using the names of family members to prescribe himself pills. He recounts, "I found myself taking more and more pills just to keep up, and then even more pills to get me to sleep again. I gave little thought to this drug use. After all, I was no street junkie making covert deals in dark alleys. I was a good doctor, with many patients, using my medical knowledge to make the path toward success a bit smoother. So I thought."[5]

His denial came to an end as the world crumbled around him. He could no longer practice medicine, and his reputation was tarnished by an investigation by the Drug Enforcement Administration concerning fraudulent prescriptions. The doctor came to terms with his prescription addiction and sought treatment. He experienced profound personal, public, and professional humiliation, which he claims followed him long after his recovery.

The Symptoms of Addiction

Many of the symptoms of addiction are similar whether a person is addicted to drugs, gambling, or social media. Denial is a classic symptom of addiction. Addicts often selectively ignore negative information in order to maintain a positive self-image and continue their behavior or substance use. If they objectively evaluated the consequences of their actions, they would need to accept responsibility for those actions, seek help, and stop doing those things. But addicts are masters of deception. They do not have a realistic view of themselves or their actions. To further their own distorted self-image, addicts make excuses for their own behavior and often cast blame on others.

There are many other common symptoms of addiction. Loss of self-control, obsession, and failed attempts to quit are common behaviors of addicts. Addicts might also exhibit feelings of guilt and shame. They often lie and miss work, school, or significant events. Fighting with friends and family, sleep disturbances, and a lack of personal care are also common among addicts.

A universal symptom of addiction is the desire to use the substance or engage in the behavior despite devastating effects. An addicted person will do harmful things to stimulate the reward center in the brain. When this area is stimulated, there is a release of dopamine that makes people feel good. In someone who is not an addict, dopamine is released in natural circumstances, such as during exercise or while listening to music. In an addict, the pleasure center is taken over by the desire to use the drugs or engage in the behavior.

During the 1950s, two researchers at McGill University in Canada conducted experiments on rats that shed light on this aspect of addiction. The researchers wanted to find out how far

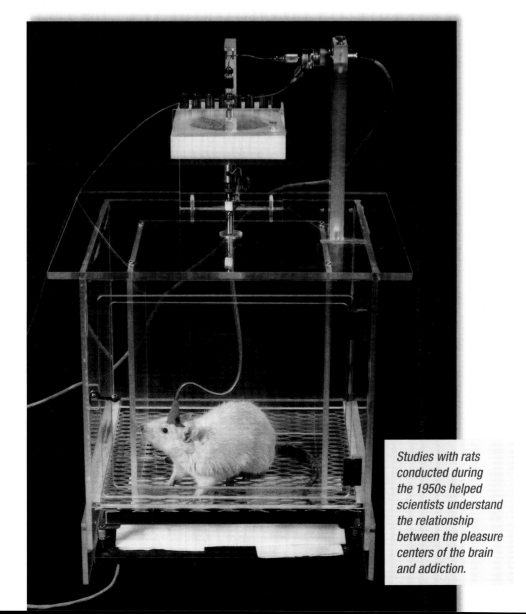

Studies with rats conducted during the 1950s helped scientists understand the relationship between the pleasure centers of the brain and addiction.

a rat would go to stimulate the pleasure center of the brain. To that end, they implanted electrodes into the rats' brains. When the rats pressed a lever, they received a tiny jolt of electricity. This jolt stimulated the brain's pleasure center. But this also had a downside: the desire for continuous pleasure caused some of the rats to push the lever up to two thousand times per hour. They stopped eating. They stopped sleeping. Some died. In their desperation for pleasure, the rats were repeatedly behaving in a way that was detrimental to their well-being.

A parallel can be drawn with people who compulsively shop, eat, gamble, and use substances. People who engage in these behaviors sometimes get sick, hurt family members, put themselves in dangerous situations, and exhaust financial resources, but most of them continue to push the lever—using the substance, eating the food, or making the next bet.

Types of Behavioral Addictions

The rat experiment simulated a behavioral addiction. The rats experienced the pleasure sensation even though they were not using a substance. There is some debate about what constitutes a behavioral addiction. Consider a teenager who checks her Instagram account every ten minutes throughout the day. It meets part of the definition of addiction in that she clearly has an overwhelming desire to look at social media. If the teenager's compulsive Instagram scrolling was happening at school and her grades were suffering, she was getting in trouble with her teachers, and it was detrimental to her self-esteem, then obsessively checking Instagram might be an addiction for this particular teenager. The Addiction Center reports that an estimated 5 to 10 percent of Americans have a social media addiction.

Many of these behaviors are socially accepted when they occur in moderation. Social media use and gambling are prime examples. Many Americans fill out a bracket for the National Collegiate Athletic Association's (NCAA) basketball tournament (known as March Madness) and bet money on the outcome. The American Gaming As-

Nicotine Addiction: Teens and Vaping

According to the 2019 National Youth Tobacco Study, more than 5 million middle and high school students use e-cigarettes. Yet many of these teens do not know the risks of vaping. In a 2018 survey from Truth Initiative, a nonprofit public health organization whose focus is ending tobacco use, 63 percent of respondents ages fifteen through twenty-four were unaware that e-cigarettes always contain nicotine. Nicotine is highly addictive. Like any other drug, it affects the brain's reward system, and the effect for people younger than twenty-five is even more significant because their brains are still developing. Many teens do not seem to be worried though. Eighteen-year-old Ben Webb tells the *Salt Lake Tribune*, "It could end up being—in the long run—really bad for us, but I just don't see it as likely. If you want to [vape], then I just don't really see anything wrong with it."

As with any addiction, addicts often do not recognize that they even have a problem until they reach bottom and try to make a change. It is only at that point that many realize the extreme challenges of kicking their addiction. "Adolescents don't think they will get addicted to nicotine," Yale neuroscientist Marina Picciotto explains, "but when they do want to stop, they find it's very difficult."

Quoted in Benjamin Wood, "They've Been Warned to Stop Vaping, but These Utahns Say They're Not Worried," *Salt Lake Tribune* (Salt Lake City, NV), December 15, 2019. www.sltrib.com.

Quoted in Kathleen Raven, "Nicotine Addiction from Vaping Is a Bigger Problem than Teens Realize," Yale Medicine, March 19, 2019. www.yalemedicine.org.

sociation estimated that 47 million Americans placed wagers totaling about $8.5 billion on the 2019 tournament. Many places of employment and social organizations even encourage people to participate. G&A Partners, a human resources consulting firm, recommends that employers embrace March Madness because it facilitates camaraderie and employee engagement. But there is a dark side to March Madness betting. Jessica Bies, a reporter for Delaware's *News Journal*, writes, "Sports betting may be exhilarating, but, for some, [it] could be the gateway to a life-changing addiction."[6]

Gambling does not always lead to addiction. For some people, betting money on the NCAA's annual March Madness basketball tournament is an enjoyable once-a-year diversion.

This was the case for Michael Pruser. When he was sixteen years old, Pruser convinced his father to bet $200 on Duke University via an online gambling account for March Madness. Pruser writes, "Unfortunately for me, I was right and I felt an adrenaline rush a 16 year old has no business feeling. It was the beginning of the end." He continued to compulsively bet on sports when he was in college. His gambling addiction grew, causing his grades to suffer. He explains, "I started skipping random classes because there was a day baseball game on TV. $50 bets turned into $100 bets. $100 bets turned into $200 bets. $200 bets turned into $500 bets."[7] By the time Pruser finished college, he had wagered an esti-

"I started skipping random classes because there was a day baseball game on TV. $50 bets turned into $100 bets. $100 bets turned into $200 bets. $200 bets turned into $500 bets."[7]

—Michael Pruser, a gambling addict

mated $5 million, was deep in debt with student loans, had no job in sight, and had a considerable gambling addiction.

Similar to gambling, gaming is also pervasive in society. From June 2018 to March 2019, 125 million new players registered for the popular video game *Fortnite*, putting the total number of players at nearly 250 million worldwide. Many parents are concerned that their children are spending too much time playing video games. Psychologist Randy Kulman had a teenage patient who averaged about forty hours of *Fortnite* per week. Kulman writes, "His mother reported that he wasn't getting out of his room very much and that he had disengaged from others, was less responsive to limit setting, and had lost interest in other activities—all symptoms of addiction."[8] In some circumstances, it seems that gaming moves beyond an activity one chooses to do for leisure into something much more harmful.

This was the case with Michael and Iana Straw, who were arrested for neglecting their twenty-two-month-old son and eleven-month-old daughter. The couple from Reno, Nevada, were too obsessively drawn to online video games, particularly *Dungeons & Dragons*, to care for their children. Michael, an unemployed cashier at the time, had used a $50,000 inheritance to purchase computer equipment and a large plasma television. When social workers took the children to the hospital, they were severely malnourished. Hospital staff had to shave the girl's hair because it was matted with cat urine. Her brother had difficulty walking due to a lack of muscle development. Regarding this case, prosecutor Kelli Ann Viloria stated, "While child abuse because of drug addiction is common, abuse rooted in video game addiction is rare."[9]

"His mother reported that he wasn't getting out of his room very much and that he had disengaged from others, was less responsive to limit setting, and had lost interest in other activities—all symptoms of addiction."[8]

—Randy Kulman, a psychologist, on his teenage patient's *Fortnite* addiction

Opioid Addiction

There are many cases of child neglect associated with substance addiction. Those substances are especially addictive because they hijack the brain's reward pathway. A substance user develops a tolerance and needs to use an increasing amount to achieve the desired effects of the substance. The Center on Addiction reports that one in seven Americans ages twelve and older (40 million people) have a substance addiction—defined as an addiction to nicotine, alcohol, or other drugs.

Opioid addiction, in particular, has become an epidemic in the United States. Opioids are drugs that contain or are derived from opium, but they also include synthetic drugs created to have the same effects. These include heroin and many different prescription drugs, which are intended for temporary use to suppress pain. Opioids relax the user, stimulate pleasure sensations, and are highly addictive. Many people have developed addictions to opioid painkillers by accident. They may have experienced a painful injury as a result of a car crash or a fall that then required medication to alleviate the pain. The Substance Abuse and Mental Health Services Administration reports that 80 percent of opioid and opiate abuse began with a legitimate prescription for medication.

This was Jason's experience. At age thirty, Jason had a debilitating snowboarding accident that left him in pain and unable to work. He began using opioids when a doctor friend prescribed them to him to ease his back pain. As time progressed, his need for pain relief increased. He began using the opioid pain relievers fentanyl and Vicodin. Then, the unthinkable happened one Christmas Eve—his wife and daughters found him unresponsive in their home. His chest was covered in fentanyl patches, and he had taken a handful of Vicodin. Paramedics treated Jason for an overdose and rushed him to the hospital. He was not expected to survive, but he did. When his wife came to pick him up eight days later, the doctor noted how fortunate he was. "You should

Cell Phone Addiction

Many experts believe that the compulsive extent to which people use their smartphones, and the ways that usage affects the brain, parallels addictive behaviors. Researchers from the Center on Addiction have proposed four criteria to identify a cell phone addiction. First, there is a disproportionate amount of time and money spent on phone usage. Second, addicts use phones in socially inappropriate or dangerous situations, such as texting while driving. Third, people with cell phone addictions might experience negative effects on their personal relationships. Finally, cell phone addicts are likely to experience anxiety when they do not have access to their phone or cell phone service. This behavior parallels withdrawal in a substance addict.

When Kevin Roose began to track his usage, he realized that he picked up his phone 101 times and spent five hours and thirty-seven minutes on his phone in a day. When he decided that he wanted to get his phone usage under control, he considered how often he used it and why. Sometimes he even used his phone for the two seconds it took for the credit card machine to run his number during a purchase. He began deleting apps on his phone to lessen its appeal. Roose writes, "Mostly, I became aware of how profoundly uncomfortable I am with stillness. For years, I've used my phone every time I've had a spare moment in an elevator or a boring meeting. . . . If I was going to repair my brain, I needed to practice doing nothing."

Kevin Roose, "How I Ditched My Phone and Unbroke My Brain," *New York Times*, February 23, 2019. www .nytimes.com.

be dead," the doctor remarked. "Your beautiful wife here should be planning your funeral."[10]

Sometimes opioid addicts do die. In April 2016, the world was stunned to learn that musician and pop culture icon Prince had died from a fentanyl overdose. The Centers for Disease Control and Prevention (CDC) reports that in 2019 more than sixty-seven thousand people died from drug overdoses. The majority of those deaths involved a prescription or illicit opioid.

The Resurgence of Meth

Methamphetamine is another drug that has destroyed millions of lives. In January 2020, the CDC found that in some states, such as Oklahoma, meth was responsible for more deaths than all opioids combined. Meth is a highly addictive drug that affects the central nervous system. It is smoked, injected, swallowed, or snorted. Someone on meth feels alert, is energized, and can stay awake for long periods of time. People addicted to meth tend to chase that high, using the drug again and again. Judith Grisel, a renowned behavioral scientist and recovering addict, describes her friend who has a meth addiction. She writes, "She'd swear off the drug, regretting that she'd spent the money she needed to buy her daughter a birthday present. . . . She'd even go so far as to block the dealer's number. But inevitably—most often on a biweekly basis that coincided with a paycheck—she'd eventually succumb to her addiction."[11]

Meth addiction is usually insurmountable without inpatient re-habilitation. Its use has catastrophic health effects. As blood pres-

Methamphetamine users, like this teenage girl, may snort, smoke, or inject the drug. Meth is one the most highly addictive and dangerous drugs that exist.

sure skyrockets, users risk having ruptured aortas and strokes. Meth use also results in extreme weight loss, sores all over the face and body, rotten teeth (referred to as "meth mouth"), dull skin, paranoia, loss of sleep, mood swings, violence, and hallucinations. Rose, a homeless seventeen-year-old in Oklahoma, told the *New York Times* in December 2019 that after a twenty-four-hour meth binge, she hallucinated so vividly that she almost jumped off a bridge.

Hallucinations are not uncommon, because the potency of meth has become stronger over time. Beginning in the 1990s, meth became widely available. It was fairly easy to make and was less expensive than cocaine. It was often manufactured with pseudoephedrine (the main ingredient in many cold medicines) in small home labs, primarily in rural areas. Meth today, however, is manufactured in labs operated by Mexican cartels and is much stronger. As Dr. Jason Beaman, the chair of psychiatry and behavioral sciences at the Center for Health Sciences at Oklahoma State University, explains, "It's way different from the meth people were using 20 years ago. It's like they were drinking Mountain Dew and now they are injecting Red Bull."[12]

Research is finding that meth use is on the rise. According to the 2017 National Survey on Drug Use and Health, approximately 1.6 million people reported having used methamphetamine during the past year. An estimated 964,000 people aged twelve or older had a methamphetamine use disorder, up from 684,000 the year prior.

Overlapping Addictions

Many addicts suffer from more than one addiction. Some people use meth to counter the effects of fentanyl, and vice versa. Whereas meth is an upper, fentanyl is a downer, so many addicts use them together. Meth brings addicts up from the lows, and fentanyl brings them down from the highs. Regarding this dangerous overlap, Dr. Brett P. Giroir, the assistant secretary for health at the US Department of Health and Human Services, says, "We definitely want to dissuade people from the notion that somehow a downer and an upper cancel each other out. Early data suggests the combination is probably more deadly than the sum of its parts."[13]

Another common pairing is alcoholism and gambling addiction. Problematic gambling is more common in people who have an alcohol use disorder. In December 2019, Alcohol Rehab Guide reported that 20 percent of people with an alcohol disorder also have a gambling addiction. Meanwhile, 73.2 percent of gambling addicts have an alcohol use disorder. Alcohol lowers inhibitions, perhaps leading to higher wagers. Higher bets and losses might lead to alcohol consumption to numb the sting. The cycle can be detrimental to one's health and financial security. Alcohol and gambling addiction each have their own sets of problems, but when they coexist, the consequences can be catastrophic.

Overlapping addictions are a logical phenomenon, given that addicts are behaving in a way to stimulate the brain's reward center. Addiction changes the brain's wiring. By repeatedly triggering the brain's reward system (through the release of dopamine), addicts do not experience reward to the extent they normally would with regular activity, such as exercise. Eventually, the addict craves, at all costs, the preferred drug or behavior just to feel normal.

Why Do People Develop Addictions?

Although some people still believe addiction is a choice, research overwhelmingly shows that addiction is a disease. Addiction rewires the brain by hijacking its reward system—and it can happen to anyone. Still, people need to consume the substance or engage in the behavior before it can become an addiction. Moreover, a mix of factors—such as genetics, exposure, choices at an early age, and the role of industry—influence the likelihood of becoming an addict.

Sometimes, family members whose lives have been uprooted by an addict have difficulty accepting the idea that addiction is a brain disease. J.D. Vance, the author of *Hillbilly Elegy* (the acclaimed memoir that explores social isolation, poverty, and addiction in America's poor white communities), grew up with a mother who was addicted to prescription narcotics. He and his sister were subjected to years of neglect and a revolving door of their mother's boyfriends. When Vance was thirteen years old, he experienced a particularly humiliating episode. His mother walked outside one day and stood in their front yard in Middletown, Ohio—dressed only in a bath towel. Intoxicated on a cocktail of prescription pills and alcohol, she was screaming at her children and other bystanders before police officers arrived and put her in their patrol car. When Vance's mother subsequently returned from rehab, she explained to her son that he should not judge her for her actions any more than he would judge a cancer patient for a tumor. He writes, "I found this patently absurd, and Mom and I often argued over whether her newfound wisdom was scientific truth or an excuse for people whose decisions destroyed a family."[14]

Genetics

Vance's mother was correct in the sense that addiction takes over the reward center of the brain. This is a big part of what keeps people addicted. Why they become addicted in the first place, however, does not have a single, simple answer. One contributing factor is a genetic predisposition, or an increased likelihood of developing addiction based on a person's genetic makeup. Ac-

Genes, which are passed from parents to children, determine traits such as height, hair color, and eye color. Many researchers believe that genes can contribute to a person's susceptibility to addiction.

cording to the American Psychological Association, 60 percent of a person's susceptibility to addiction is attributable to his or her genes. Genes, which pass from parents to children, carry the information that determines characteristics such as height and eye color. Researchers believe that some people also inherit genes that make them more likely to become addicts. In fact, researchers have identified fifty genes that might contribute to addiction vulnerability. Even with this information, they do not fully understand the role genetics plays in addiction.

People who are genetically predisposed to addiction might face harsher consequences for their choices to experiment with drugs and alcohol. "We need to tell our children that one drink or one pill can lead to an addiction," warns Maxine, who works for the addiction crisis organization Shatterproof. "Some of us have the genes that increase our risk of addiction, even after just a few uses."[15] According to the organization Addiction Treatment Services, some people inherit genes that cause them to experience more extreme withdrawal symptoms, heightened pleasure from certain behaviors or substances, and more difficulty refraining from substances or behaviors.

> "We need to tell our children that one drink or one pill can lead to an addiction. Some of us have the genes that increase our risk of addiction, even after just a few uses."[15]
>
> —Maxine, an ambassador with Shatterproof

The Home Environment

Genetics is only one factor in addiction. Home environment is another. A study conducted by the Department of Epidemiology and Public Health at Yale University School of Medicine concluded that the children of addicts are eight times more likely to become addicts themselves. However, having an addicted parent does not automatically mean a child will become an addict; rather, there are factors that make it more likely.

The National Institute on Drug Abuse estimates that 25 percent of children in the United States grow up in households where there is substance abuse. Experts note that children learn from their parents, often adopting the behaviors they see at an early age. They are also more likely to have access to illicit substances in their homes. In some cases, they develop unhealthy ways of coping with their parents' addictions.

This is what happened to Katie Haupt. Her father was addicted to drugs and alcohol when she was a child. When under the influence, he had violent outbursts that Haupt thought were a normal part of life. When Haupt grew older, she ate and shopped compulsively. She explains,

> When things got really crazy, my mom would say, "Oh let's go shopping." To escape. To get away from this, let's cover it up and pretend it's OK by doing that. It wasn't until later that I realized that it's not healthy to cover up pain. You have to kind of figure it out, deal with it, face that pain, instead of burying it. . . . That's why people get addicted, because they get addicted to not feeling pain.[16]

Like Haupt and many others whose parents are addicts, their experiences from childhood often affect their subsequent life choices.

Poor Choices at a Young Age

Anyone can make poor choices, but some teens are more prone to making poor choices than others. For example, teens who are less supervised and have parents who are alcoholics might have more opportunity or inclination to become intoxicated because they are able to come home unnoticed. Using drugs and engaging in risky behaviors is never advisable, but doing so at a young age has even more detrimental consequences than it would later in life. According to the Center on Addiction, one in four Ameri-

Addicted from Birth

Children who are exposed to substances before they are born are sometimes at an even more substantial disadvantage from the very beginning. The National Center on Substance Abuse and Child Welfare estimates that 15 percent of babies born each year have been exposed to alcohol or illicit drugs in utero. This comes with a host of developmental and health problems for the substance-exposed babies. For example, prenatal exposure to cocaine leads to an increased risk of depression, heart disease, seizures, schizophrenia, and Parkinson's disease in adulthood. Prenatal exposure to heroin can lead to poor spatial recognition, poor memory recall, hyperactivity, and lower IQ. Newborn babies exposed to opioids in utero can further experience life-threatening withdrawal symptoms.

Exposure to illicit substances in utero also heightens the risk of developing addictions in the future. Studies examining the long-term effects of illicit substance exposure in utero have found that drugs affect dopamine and serotonin pathways in the brain, thereby potentially hijacking the babies, reward centers before they are born.

Finally, exposure in utero means that those children are often being raised by addicts from day one. There is hope though. Recent long-term studies of adopted children who were exposed to heroin in utero indicate that "the outcomes of children who were adopted by non-addicted parents greatly improved over those children who remained in compromised environments," according to Addiction Campuses. This means that there is promise of overcoming drug exposure; being nurtured in a healthy family environment can significantly benefit a child's health and well-being.

Addiction Campuses, "Drug Addiction and Babies: Long Term Effects," *Addiction Campuses Blog*, October 4, 2019. www.addictioncampuses.com.

cans who used an addictive substance before age eighteen became addicted. The center also notes that young people who began using addictive substances before age fifteen were almost seven times more likely to develop a substance abuse problem than those who did not use until they were over twenty-one. Of the people who have substance abuse problems in adulthood, nine in ten people started using before they were eighteen. This is not meant to suggest that people who use substances after age twenty-one are safe from addiction, but researchers have identified a clear link between addiction and early exposure.

Colten Wooten was sixteen and a high school sophomore in Raleigh, North Carolina, when he tried heroin for the first time. He had already been using amphetamines and cocaine to get high, and he thought heroin would help him ease down. By his senior year, he was using heroin every single day. By age twenty-four, Wooten had organ damage from prolonged drug use and was flirting with death from a possible overdose. At one point, after shooting up heroin all night in a stranger's apartment, he realized he was down to his last dose. At that moment, the thought occurred to him that he might die. Wooten writes, "This is how people die. They overdose in unknown company, and their bodies are shoved into coat closets in dilapidated buildings and aren't discovered for months."[17] That night, he called his mother and tried to get treatment for his addictions. His path to recovery has been troubled. Use at such a young age might have contributed to making his recovery journey that much more challenging.

> "This is how people die. They overdose in unknown company, and their bodies are shoved into coat closets in dilapidated buildings and aren't discovered for months."[17]
>
> —Colten Wooten, a drug addict since age sixteen

The Video Game Industry

Exposure to addictive substances and behaviors is not limited to home and family. Young people, in particular, are bombarded with products that are designed to enhance the consumer's desire for more. By successfully hooking young people on a product or substance, those companies create for themselves a steady base of lifelong customers (or, some would say, addicts). Some experts cite video games as an example. Not

Although not everyone who plays video games becomes addicted, there is some evidence that the games are addictive for many people, including teens.

everyone who plays video games is an addict. There is some evidence though, that games are addictive for many people. This addiction is fueled by elements of the games themselves. "Gaming companies are enlisting the help of PhD behavioural psychologists using state-of-the-art research and data to make their games as addictive as possible,"[18] says James Good of Game Quitters, an organization that helps people who have video game addiction.

Video games have become increasingly addictive over time. In the past, video game manufacturers would release the whole game and then create a sequel (for example, *Super Mario Bros. 1, 2,* and *3*). Now, video games are designed to keep the players engaged because there is no end. There is no way to beat the game. The player just continues to level up. There is no satisfaction in completion, only the desire to keep advancing.

The Temptation of State Lotteries

Some environmental contexts are believed to foster addiction. For compulsive gamblers, state lotteries expand the sphere of temptation. The ubiquitous presence of the ever-promising scratch-off ticket makes those predisposed more likely to gamble. Scratch-off tickets can be found at almost every gas station in forty-four states as well as in the District of Columbia. In addition to income, sales, and property taxes, states collect revenue from their lotteries. Proponents of state lotteries argue that it is a way for states to collect a harmless, voluntary tax—sometimes from out-of-state residents.

But opponents of state lotteries contend that gambling is not exactly a voluntary tax. They argue that because compulsive gambling has been recognized as an addictive disease, the reliance on gamblers to fund public services actually preys on their addictions. Furthermore, opponents argue that state gambling administrators often downplay the poor odds of winning to the point that gamblers are being tricked into these spending decisions.

Video game manufacturers use various methods to trigger the reward center of the brain, says Ramsay Brown, the cofounder of Dopamine Labs (a company that aims to increase the rate at which people use game apps). Going shopping, finding a bargain, and receiving a gift are natural ways dopamine is released in the brain. To that end, loot boxes have been introduced as a reward mechanism for that feel-good experience in video games. A loot box is a virtual reward, usually with a price tag that includes real money, containing a random item for the game. In some cases, the item is described as rare, and users are given special opportunities to buy it with their money only after they level up. Some gamers have spent their entire savings on loot boxes.

A young man who goes by the user name Kensgold says he began playing video games at age thirteen. By the time he was a sophomore in high school and was working a part-time job at a sandwich shop, he was spending 90 percent of his wages on gaming. Now nineteen, he describes a three-year period when he spent $17,827 on in-game purchases in *Counter-Strike: Global Offensive*, *Smite*, and *The Hobbit: Kingdoms of Middle-Earth*. In an open letter to publisher Electronic Arts (EA), Kensgold describes his video game addiction as a plea to the designers to understand the effects of what they are doing when they create these games. He explains, "The majority of the reason that I made my post was not really to slam EA or any of the companies that do this, but to share my story and to show that these transactions are not as innocent as they really appear to be. They can lead you down a path. It's not like buying a stick of gum at the store."[19]

Social Media: Designed for Addiction

Video games are not the only popular pastimes that have been linked to addiction. Social media is increasingly being viewed as an addictive activity. Research into the links between social media and addiction is relatively new, but already some work shows that many social media users are addicts or are becoming addicted. According to a 2019 Global Web Index Survey, internet users are spending an average of two hours and twenty-two minutes per day on social media. Teens spend even more time than that. They are spending an increasing amount of time on screens—both for games and social media. Common Sense Media, a nonprofit organization that researches, rates, and reviews online activities for young people, found that on average, US teens spend over seven hours per day on screens for entertainment, not including time spent on screens for school and homework. The top social media sites used by teens include Instagram and TikTok, among others.

Worldwide, however, Facebook is by far the most popular of the social media platforms, and many argue that it is highly addictive. At the 2018 World Economic Forum in Davos, Switzerland, one tech industry insider compared Facebook to smoking and suggested that the social media platform should be regulated in the same way, with consumer safety valued above profits.

A 2019 survey found that internet users spend an average of two hours and twenty-two minutes per day on social media, which they often access with their smartphones.

Facebook and other social media are said to be addictive for many reasons. Humans are social creatures and long for a sense of belonging. There are many group options and chances to connect with others on social media. People need validation, and they feel validated with all of the "likes" and other emojis Facebook has to offer. Social media also gives people a platform to broadcast accomplishments and other positive things about themselves. Finally, talking or posting about oneself triggers the reward center in the brain, and social media outlets offer an easy way to do that. Social media generally is addictive for reasons that coincide with human nature. But tech experts say that Facebook engineers purposefully design and update the platform to generate frequent and continued use among its members.

Siva Vaidhyanathan, a professor of media studies and the director of the Center for Media and Citizenship at the University of Virginia, argues that Facebook intentionally uses the same techniques as a casino to keep users coming back for more. Slot machines, also known as fruit machines, found in casinos are popular among gamblers. Users insert a coin into the machine and pull a lever. If a combination of certain fruits appears, they win money. In an interview with the *Washington Post*, Vaidhyanathan explains that Facebook is "perfectly designed, like a fruit machine in a casino, to give us a tiny sliver of pleasure when we use it and introduce a small measure of anxiety when we do not use it. A Facebook user says, 'What am I missing out on? Did anyone "like" my joke?' A casino patron says, 'I wonder if THIS is my lucky moment or lucky pull of the lever.'"[20]

> "[Facebook is] perfectly designed . . . to give us a tiny sliver of pleasure when we use it and introduce a small measure of anxiety when we do not use it."[20]
>
> —Siva Vaidhyanathan, the director of the Center for Media and Citizenship at the University of Virginia

Although not all social media users are addicts, Facebook's tactics are attracting widespread use. There are nearly 2.4 billion active monthly Facebook users. In the United States, 68 percent of adults use Facebook, half of them several times a day. The Pew Research Center found that 51 percent of teens use Facebook as well. In 2019, Facebook was the fourth most-valuable brand in the world, valued at $94.8 billion.

A Mix of Factors

A combination of factors leads to addiction. Many industries design products in ways that make people stay engaged. Genetic coding, including the interaction of up to fifty genes, influences how a person will deal with the desire to use a product or substance or to engage in a behavior, as well as his or her ability not to use or engage. Chance and circumstance play a significant role in a person's predisposition for addiction as well. Some children might live in a house where they frequently see lines of cocaine laid out on mirrors and snorted by parents before the children are in secondary school. Others might not ever see cocaine or be offered it at all. These factors and many more interact as characters in the addiction story.

Chapter Three

Ruined Lives

In October 2019, Erika Hurt's Facebook post went viral. In the post, Hurt is pictured next to her three-year-old son, Parker, holding a sign that reads, "Narcan saved my life." Her son also holds a sign: "And now I get to have my mommy."[21] It marked Hurt's three-year anniversary of sobriety. Before that social media post, Hurt was known for a widely posted picture taken by a police officer that showed her overdosing in the front seat of her car; in the photo, she holds a hypodermic needle in her hand while her infant son cries in the backseat. Medics who arrived at the scene in an Indiana parking lot saved her life when they administered two doses of Narcan, which reversed the overdose, and rushed her to the hospital. The overdose picture illustrated the nation's opioid addiction problem, but it came at Hurt's expense. She was humiliated and feared that her son would be taken away from her.

Her fears were not unfounded. Following the incident, Hurt spent two months in jail and six months in a court-ordered rehab program. When Hurt's mother and son visited, her son did not know her. In her 2019 Facebook post, she wrote, "Millions saw me overdose after a photo taken of me by a police officer went viral. None of those people have seemed to have time to reach out and check on me, so here is an update: Today I celebrated three years clean and my son gets to have his mommy back. How about you make THAT go viral!"[22]

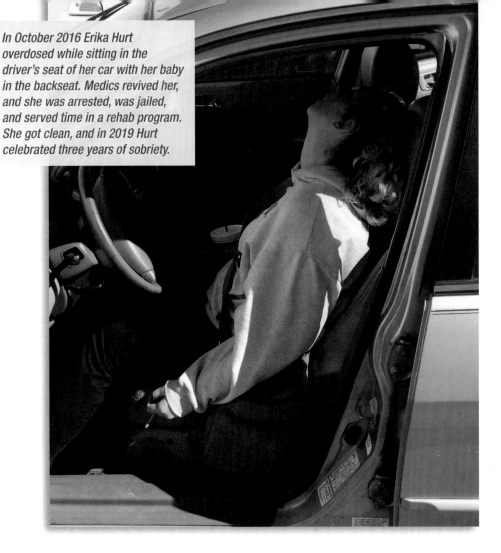

In October 2016 Erika Hurt overdosed while sitting in the driver's seat of her car with her baby in the backseat. Medics revived her, and she was arrested, was jailed, and served time in a rehab program. She got clean, and in 2019 Hurt celebrated three years of sobriety.

Overdose

Erika Hurt is not alone in her substance addiction problem. The Center on Addiction reports that one in seven Americans ages twelve and older (40 million people) have substance addictions. A drug overdose is one of the clearest and most severe consequences of addiction. The CDC reports that from 1999 to 2017, more than 702,000 people died from drug overdoses. The number of drug overdose deaths per year increased every year from 1999, when there were 16,849 deaths, to 2017, when that number reached 70,237. In 2018, drug overdose deaths decreased by 4 percent, and some experts are hopeful that this marks the beginning of a downward trend.

West Virginia has the highest rate of drug overdose deaths in the United States, 49.6 per 100,000 people. That is three times higher than the national average. In August 2016 alone, 26 people overdosed in Huntington, West Virginia, during a four-hour period. Some speculate that a strong batch of heroin caused the string of overdoses. Others think that users had received a batch of heroin laced with fentanyl, a synthetic opioid that is much stronger than heroin. Either way, the many overdoses in a short time period highlight the pervasiveness of drug addiction in the small Appalachian community.

Officials estimate that about 10 percent of the population of Huntington, West Virginia, abuse opioids. Following the massive overdose episode in August 2016, community leaders in Huntington used $1.2 million from federal grants to begin a program involving quick-response teams. Each team, which includes a paramedic, police officers, and a religious leader, visits people who have recently overdosed. They tell addicts about clean needle programs, give out medicine to reverse overdoses, and share information on treatment programs. Connie Priddy, a registered nurse with Cabell County Emergency Medical Services who coordinates the program, says, "We leave them our information. We'll go back a couple of days later and talk to them again. We'll call them; we'll text them. So if they're not ready, they're not ready — but we keep going back."[23]

Teen Overdose Deaths

Teen deaths from drug overdoses are also on the rise. While overall teen drug use is lower now than it has been in recent years (according to the Monitoring the Future Survey), overdose deaths (3.7 deaths for every 100,000 teens) are up. Heroin and fentanyl use are to blame. In separate incidents in September 2019 near Seattle, Washington, three teens accidentally overdosed on fentanyl. All three reportedly believed they were taking the prescription painkiller oxycodone. Keven Wynkoop, the principal of Ballard High School, where one of the teens attended, sent a letter home to parents that read, "I am asking that you have a direct conversation with your child/children about the pills and the extreme danger of using illegal substances. Fentanyl, even in very small doses, is likely to lead to death."[24]

Seventeen-year-old Gabe Lilienthal was one of the Seattle area's sixty-five fentanyl deaths in 2019. Deborah Savran, Lilienthal's mother, explains that he suffered from insomnia and anxiety and suggests he bought the pills to help him sleep. Lilienthal's parents use the word *poisoned* rather than *overdosed* to describe his death. His mother says, "We feel like there's a serial killer on the street. They're selling these drugs to people and it's like Russian roulette."[25]

Health Consequences

Aside from death and overdose, there are many health consequences of addiction. Substance addiction affects all systems in the body and can lead to a large variety of health problems. For example, meth use can cause teeth to rot and eventually fall out. It can also cause sores to develop all over the skin. Alcohol abuse often leads to liver damage. In many cases, smoking cigarettes causes lung cancer. Injecting heroin can lead to human immunodeficiency virus (HIV) and hepatitis C (from sharing needles) as well as infections of the heart and skin from bacteria. Likewise, behavioral addictions also have many health consequences.

This was the case with Eric McKillen, who was overcurious about sex from an early age. When he was seventeen years old, a year after he lost his virginity to his high school girlfriend, he hired a prostitute for the first time in the red-light district of Amsterdam. Despite harboring disgust for himself, he returned the following night and hired another one. By his own account, McKillen became addicted to sex, hired over two hundred sex workers, and spent $150,000 on his habit. His addiction had serious consequences. He writes,

"I have been mugged, threatened, had knives pulled on me. I have had a few car accidents rushing out for in-calls to fit my habit into a day's work schedule."[26]

McKillen also contracted chlamydia, a curable sexually transmitted disease (STD). PsychGuides.com, which provides information on psychological disorders, reports that about 38 percent of men and 45 percent of women with sex addictions have an STD. Additionally, the website explains that a survey of women with sex addictions found that 70 percent of respondents had experienced at least one unwanted pregnancy as a result of their addiction. People with behavioral addictions also commonly suffer from depression and use their addiction to numb their emotions. When McKillen cheated on a woman with whom he was in a relationship, having unprotected sex with an escort

"I have been mugged, threatened, had knives pulled on me. I have had a few car accidents rushing out for in-calls to fit my habit into a day's work schedule."[26]

—Eric McKillen, a recovering sex addict

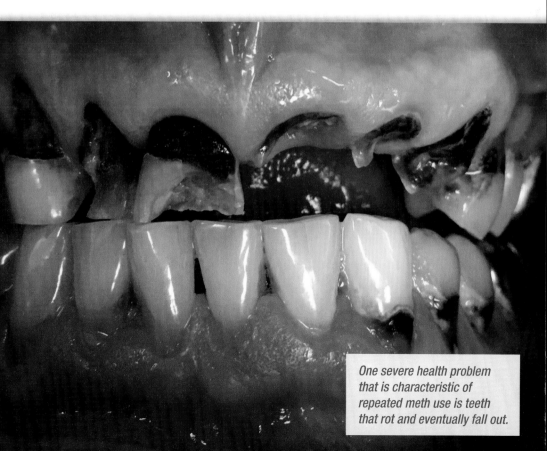

One severe health problem that is characteristic of repeated meth use is teeth that rot and eventually fall out.

and ending his relationship, he became severely depressed. He writes, "I spiraled and binged, sleeping with more prostitutes, engaging in higher-risk sex."[27] Depression and anxiety are common symptoms of both behavioral and substance addicts.

Destroyed Relationships

Like McKillen's betrayal of a girlfriend he once cherished, there are usually many destroyed relationships in every addict's wake. Leigh is a recovering addict who sacrificed his relationship with his wife and two daughters to engage in online gambling. He explains, "When I was with my family, I was physically there—but mentally, I was miles away, thinking about gambling: when I could next bet, where would the money come from, whether I could back a winner."[28] He would even place bets when walking the dog or when his daughters were in the bath.

Leigh's compulsive gambling cost him almost everything. His bets ranged from $5,000 to $20,000 a day. One evening, two large men came to his home and punched him. He owed them money, and they told him he had better pay it or next time they would return and use a baseball bat instead. The incident prompted Leigh to steal money from his work. He lost his job as a finance manager and was sentenced to a year in jail. Leigh also lost all of his belongings, including his house and car, but he says the material losses pale in comparison to the loss of his family and friends. He writes, "My marriage disintegrated, I lost access to my children, I don't talk to my family and I'm no longer on speaking terms with most of my friends. I don't blame them."[29]

> "My marriage disintegrated, I lost access to my children, I don't talk to my family and I'm no longer on speaking terms with most of my friends. I don't blame them."[29]
>
> —Leigh, a recovering gambling addict

Many addicts are like Leigh; they sacrifice almost everything for their addictions. Too often addicted parents are unfit to care for their children. A March 2019 report from the United Hospital

The Crime of Causing an Overdose

Kimberly Elkins and Aaron Rost were engaged to be married when Elkins began using fentanyl patches for chronic pain management. The need for pain relief evolved into addiction for Elkins and also her fiancé. Rather than the prescribed topical use, the couple would also ingest the gel from the patches to get high. One cold winter morning in northern Minnesota, thirty-six-year-old Rost put a piece of the patch in his mouth and overdosed before he could make it out the door to go hunting. Elkins, who had also ingested a piece of the same patch, survived and woke up in the hospital. Two months after her fiancé's funeral, Elkins was arrested and charged with third-degree murder because the patches Rost ingested had been prescribed to her. She pleaded guilty to a lesser charge—second-degree manslaughter—and was sentenced to four years in prison.

This was not an isolated case, although it is not common either. From 2015 to 2018, in the fifteen states where data was available, the *New York Times* identified one thousand cases in which a person was criminally charged with someone else's drug overdose. Prosecution is one tool among many to deter drug use and reduce addiction, say advocates of this approach. People who argue against the prosecution of these cases suggest that drug addiction is a public health crisis and should not be treated as a crime.

Fund found that from 2012 to 2019, foster care placement of children in the United States increased by 10 percent. Many experts believe that this increase is fueled by addicts caught up in the opioid epidemic. But not all children with unfit parents are removed from their situations. They are sometimes neglected and abused until there is an acute crisis in their lives that draws legal attention. In the documentary *Heroin's Children*, which draws attention to those cases, a nine-year-old speaks with a 911 operator as her mother is overdosing on heroin. The girl explains, "My mom is on the floor. . . . No, she's not awake. She's changing color." The operator says, "Keep talking to her." In response, the little girl cries, "Mom, wake up! Mom, wake up! Mom, wake up!"[30] There are too many children tragically stuck in circumstances of neglect and/or abuse because their parents are addicts. The Substance Abuse and Mental Health Services Administration reports that one in ten children in the United States lives in a household with at least one parent who has a substance abuse disorder. The majority of them are under age five.

Trauma and Homelessness

Some children with addicted parents become homeless when their parents lose the family house. The National Coalition for the Homeless has found that 38 percent of homeless people are alcohol dependent, and 26 percent are dependent on other drugs. Many of those people have children.

A January 2020 report from the National Center for Homeless Education revealed that more than 1.5 million students in public schools across the United States were homeless for some time during the 2017–2018 school year, a 15 percent increase from the previous year. Some of these students were displaced because of a fire, a hurricane, or factory shutdowns. But according to Barbara Duffield, the executive director of SchoolHouse Connection, a nonprofit supporting homeless youths, the opioid and methamphetamine addiction crises have contributed to the increase in student homelessness.

In Portsmouth, Ohio, Hannah Thurman was nine years old when she became homeless for a few weeks with her mother, Anna, an opioid addict, and two younger brothers. Hannah recalls being locked out of the family trailer for long periods of time with only water and bologna sandwiches or cold hot dogs to eat while her parents and their friends used drugs. When she was in fourth grade, her mother's boyfriend came into their trailer and killed Hannah's father with a shotgun. Hannah remembers holding towels to his stomach wounds before he died. During his funeral, her mother left with her friend to get high.

More than 1.5 million students in US public schools were homeless at some point during the 2017–2018 school year. Experts say the opioid and methamphetamine crises have contributed to student homelessness.

Shortly after Hannah's dad's death, the Thurman family lost their home. For the next three weeks, they moved from house to house and to a motel known for drug use. When Hannah told her school guidance counselor that she was considering killing herself, officials began making emergency custody arrangements with an aunt and uncle for Hannah and her brothers. Their mother, still frequently using opioids, fought for custody. Hannah's aunt and uncle were forced to get a restraining order against her.

Years have passed, and Hannah and her brothers are still living with their aunt and uncle. About her aunt and uncle, Hannah told the *New York Times*, "They're my safe place. I don't have to be scared anymore."[31]

The consequences of addiction are often crystal clear. Hannah's parents abused substances, creating an unstable life for their children. The children experienced trauma and homelessness before finding comfort and stability with their aunt and uncle. In the case of Leigh, the gambling addict, he owed money, stole from work, lost his job, and was sentenced to jail.

The Other Costs of Addiction

Sometimes the economic costs and loss of productivity resulting from addiction are less clear-cut. Over a fifteen-year period from 2000 to 2015, men in their twenties without a college degree were increasingly likely to be unemployed, live with their parents, and remain unmarried. In 2016, 15 percent of men ages twenty-one to thirty were not working or in full-time education, up from 8 percent in 2000. The number of hours young men worked during this time declined more significantly than that of their older counterparts.

During the same period, video games became more entertaining, affordable, and arguably, addictive. In March 2017, *The Economist* reported that each hour that the group did not work, leisure time increased by an hour. Of that leisure time, 75 percent involved gaming. Cause-and-effect relationships here are not completely clear. Maybe young men had a more difficult time finding jobs, housing prices increased, and gaming became their new hobby. Many experts speculate, however, that gaming addiction has left a large group of young men unmotivated, unemployed, and living in their parents' basements.

"It felt so much easier to go home, flip a switch and play a game."[32]

—Tim Walrod, a recovering gaming addict

Narcan and the Proposed Three-Strikes Rule

In May 2017, a five-year-old boy walked barefoot for two blocks in Middletown, Ohio, to a relative's house to announce that his parents were dead. First responders rushed to the boy's home and revived his parents from heroin overdoses. Middletown, with a population of fifty thousand people, has been so plagued with heroin overdoses that a city councilman proposed a three-strikes rule. Under this rule, emergency medical responders would only be allowed to revive a heroin addict twice from an overdose. The third time, the addict would be on his or her own.

For Councilman Dan Picard, the incident with the five-year-old was the last straw. Picard and others were frustrated that drug addiction seemed to be exhausting the city's resources, with no end in sight. City Manager Douglas Adkins, who did not weigh in on the proposal, argued, "We can't arrest our way out of this. I can't keep it out of the city. It's a Middletown problem. It's a southwest Ohio problem. It's an Ohio problem. It's a national epidemic." Critics saw the proposed law as cold and inhumane, but it did reflect the town's frustration over the continuing costs of addiction. The proposed law was ultimately rejected.

Quoted in John Bacon, "Ohio Councilman: After Two Overdoses, No More EMS," *USA Today*, June 28, 2017. www.usatoday.com.

Tim Walrod, a twenty-eight-year-old from California, almost missed his chance to go to nursing school because of his video game addiction. Walrod tells the *New York Post* that rather than dealing with reality, "it felt so much easier to go home, flip a switch and play a game."[32] Walrod would avoid his problems by playing *World of Warcraft* for eight hours at a time. When he missed the deadline to apply for nursing school, he realized he had a significant problem. He was unemployed at that time and dreaded telling his mom that he had been playing games and missed the important deadline. Over time, he quit gaming and has since replaced it with other interests like meditation, guitar lessons, learning Spanish, and running. After giving up video games, he was also admitted to and completed nursing school.

Learning from Addiction

Addiction can do many things. It steals time, harms or kills people, takes homes and jobs, and breaks families apart. But in the best-case scenarios, it acts as a productive teacher. It shows people whom they do not want to be or, as in Hannah's case, whom they do not want to emulate.

Chapter Four

Crime and Punishment

While people from at least six different households were on vacation or at work, a thirty-five-year-old homeless heroin addict broke into their homes to steal jewelry, electronics, and other things of value. According to the 2018 Narconon report (which did not name the city or state), the addict stole an estimated $7,000 worth of goods. Narconon is an international drug rehabilitation program that also collects and presents data on substance addiction. Some areas fighting community heroin addictions are facing a 30 percent increase in residential burglaries from the year prior. The annual cost of drug-related crime in the United States is $61 billion. Drug addicts, desperate for their next fix, will sometimes do whatever it takes to get the money to buy their drug of choice.

Addiction and crime go hand in hand. Addicts develop powerful needs, both physical and emotional. These needs, when not met, often lead to desperation—and desperate people will do many things that they might not have done otherwise. Experts say that addiction lies at the heart of many crimes. Joseph A. Shrand, a professor of psychiatry at Harvard Medical School, argues in *Psychology Today*, "Addiction is not a crime but can lead to them."[33]

Getting Money for a Gambling Habit

Theft is a common crime committed by addicts. Gamblers, for instance, sometimes steal when they have exhausted their own money and are in danger of not being able to keep up their routine. Sixty-year-old Kathleen Pasch stole more than $100,000 for her gambling habit from the Black Creek Rescue Service while she served as the organization's treasurer. According to the criminal complaint filed in July 2019 in Outagamie County, Wisconsin, Pasch "admitted that she had a gambling problem and that she had taken funds . . . to support her addiction. She acknowledged that what she did was wrong and claimed that she always intended to repay the money that she stole."[34]

Theft is not unusual for a gambling addict. Rose Blozinski, the executive director of the Wisconsin Council on Problem Gambling, explains that stealing is a pervasive problem for many gamblers. She says, "They don't start out losing large sums. They gamble

Drug-related crime in the United States costs a staggering $61 billion per year. Drug addicts who are desperate for their next fix may do whatever it takes to get the money they need to buy drugs.

for fun and then it becomes a problem. They intend to pay it back, but they get deeper in, and they fall behind."[35] A Georgia State University survey of gambling addicts involved in the recovery program Gamblers Anonymous found that the people who reported stealing each took an average of $135,000 in either money or property.

> "They don't start out losing large sums. They gamble for fun and then it becomes a problem. They intend to pay it back, but they get deeper in, and they fall behind."[35]
>
> —Rose Blozinski, the executive director of the Wisconsin Council on Problem Gambling

Addicted Prostitutes

Addicts commit crimes other than burglary and theft to get resources for their addictions. Some women engage in illegal sex work, or prostitution, because they need to earn money to live. Others do it in exchange for drugs or for money for drugs. Beth is an example of the latter. She had supportive parents, refrained from drugs and alcohol in high school, and got her diploma in Huntington, West Virginia. She would seem an unlikely candidate for prostitution. When she was nineteen, her friend Amber gave her an 80-milligram tablet of the opioid painkiller oxycodone to get high. Beth says it was all downhill from there. She began trading sex for drugs. Five years later, Beth was addicted to opioids and was prostituting herself on the streets of Huntington. Other women have done the same, often with encouragement from a pimp who vows to keep the drugs flowing. Assistant US Attorney Andrew Cogar explains that "pimps often hold out [the] promise of drugs in return for women engaging in prostitution. We think that's fueling a lot of the demand and supply."[36]

Prostitutes trading sex for drugs are even more likely to be subjected to violence than other addicts are. They suffer fates worse than incarceration even before they are caught. In 2019, an anonymous sex addict wrote an article in which he detailed his more than twenty-year solicitation of drug-addicted prostitutes. He wrote, "Nearly every woman with whom I associated would

Shoplifting is not just a crime. For some people, it is also an addiction. According to the National Association for Shoplifting Prevention (NASP), as of 2019, one in eleven Americans had committed the crime of shoplifting in their lifetime. Some of them do it compulsively, meaning they have an overwhelming urge to steal items from a store, a friend's house, school, their mother's purse, and anywhere else they are afforded the opportunity. In 2019, American Retail Supply reported that the most commonly stolen nonfood items included cosmetics, jewelry, handbags, cigarettes, razors, and deodorant.

Few shoplifting addicts steal items out of necessity. Most do it for the adrenaline rush they get from illegally taking the items. This applies, in particular, to teens. In addition to adrenaline, teens usually steal because of peer pressure and as an act of rebellion. Peter Berlin, NASP's founder, says kids shoplift "because they wanted nice things, felt pressured by friends, wanted to see if they could get away with it, or were angry, depressed, confused or bored. Sometimes they are just mad at the world and want to strike back."

Many people who compulsively shoplift are trying to regain control over something. As Terry Shulman, a recovering shoplifter and the founder of Kleptomaniacs and Shoplifters Anonymous, explains, "Some start after a loss, trauma, betrayal, or some difficult transition in their life. . . . I was making life right by taking something life had taken from me. I didn't know that at the time, but that was very powerful in a way. It was symbolic and through repetition it got to be a real habit."

Quoted in Samantha Morton, "The Deal on Why Teens Steal," Metro Parent, April 8, 2019. www.metroparent.com.

Quoted in Cory Stieg, "What Trinkets Gets Wrong and Right About Shopping Addiction," Refinery29, June 14, 2019. www.refinery29.com.

tell me stories of men who beat them, robbed them or abandoned them. One woman was stabbed. None went to the authorities. The buyers know this, and it encourages aggressive behavior."[37] He further explained that these women were suspicious of police because they did not want to be caught and arrested for possession of illegal drugs or for prostitution.

Drug Manufacturing, Robbery, and Theft

Aside from selling sex for their substance addictions, addicts also have been known to take other desperate measures—manufacturing, distributing, and trafficking illicit substances–to get drugs for personal use. For the past couple of decades, rural areas in the United States in particular have been plagued by makeshift methamphetamine labs. They usually involve the use of flammable liquids and containers heated over open flames. The labs are illegal and dangerous, and many people working inside them have died or been severely burned when the labs blew up. Still, meth addicts, desperate for their next high, are willing to risk everything to get the drug. They make the meth in labs and then sell it to other addicts.

Sometimes, prison is not a deterrent. In Massachusetts in 2014, thirty-eight-year-old Edward Rooney was sentenced to four to six years in prison for possessing meth with the intent to distribute. In February 2020, after having served time in prison, Rooney died following a meth lab explosion in his apartment on Cape Cod. Neighbors woke to him screaming for help outside of their home following the explosion. They let him into their mudroom, where he collapsed moments later. Paramedics took him to the hospital, where he died shortly afterward.

Opioid addicts further have resorted to robbing pharmacies to get prescription drugs. In January 2020, three men in Palo Alto, California, robbed a Safeway pharmacy for prescription pills. One of the trio allegedly held a gun and demanded that the worker get on the ground. The second man broke the glass door of the pharmacy and stole prescription drugs. The third acted as a lookout. When they had finished stealing the drugs, the three left the scene in a pickup truck, which led authorities to their identities. Many of these pharmaceutical robberies are occurring across the country.

Some opioid addicts are abusing their professional positions to get drugs. Katrina Fahlberg, a pharmacy worker in Florida, was caught in November 2019 stealing opioid painkillers called tramadol from the pharmacy where she worked. She told her coworkers that she began stealing the pills a year earlier. The emergency suspension order of her pharmaceutical tech license stated, "Ms. Fahlberg admitted that she took the bottles of tramadol off the shelf, poured out five to ten tablets, and consumed them. Ms. Fahlberg also admitted that she concealed stolen tablets of tramadol in her bra and bottles in her purse."[38]

Prison: A Population of Addicts

Many addicts end up in prison. Drug and alcohol addictions are the most common addictions found among prison inmates. In 2020, American Addiction Centers reported that more than 65 percent of people in US prisons and jails meet the criteria for drug and alcohol addiction. Many inmates are there because of crimes fueled by their addiction. This involves crimes directly aimed at getting more drugs or more money for their addiction. A June 2017 Bureau of Justice Statistics (BJS) report finds that 21 percent of people sentenced to prison or jail in the United States are incarcerated for crimes committed to get drugs or money for drugs.

Many crimes are committed while offenders are under the influence of drugs or alcohol. The BJS states, "Drugs are . . . related to crime through the effects they have on the user's behavior and by generating violence and other illegal activity in connection with drug trafficking."[39] According to BJS data collected from victims of violent crimes, 24.2 percent of offenders arrested for violent crimes were under the influence of drugs or alcohol. The same is true for 30 percent arrested for rapes or sexual assaults and 23.3 percent arrested for robbery. The *Journal of Substance Abuse Treatment* reports that more than 75 percent of people who began substance addiction treatment report having performed acts of violence, includ-

"Drugs are . . . related to crime through the effects they have on the user's behavior and by generating violence and other illegal activity in connection with drug trafficking."[39]

—Bureau of Justice Statistics

Drug addicts often end up getting arrested and serving time in prison. According to American Addiction Centers, more than 65 percent of people in US prisons and jails are addicted to drugs and/or alcohol.

ing mugging, physical assault, and attacking another person with a weapon.

Sosha Lewis's parents were among the addicts committing acts of violence. In her local newspaper, Lewis writes, "As a 7-year-old walking home from the bus stop, I watched as my father punched my mom and then picked her up and threw her through the window in the door. . . . My parents, Steve and Starr,

When Texting Kills

Despite the abundance of research indicating the dangers of texting while driving, many people cannot resist the urge to use their phones while at the wheel. The compulsive need to retrieve a message and respond as soon as the indicator sounds—despite the danger of doing so while driving—arguably parallels addictive behavior.

Texting while driving has become a significant hazard nationwide. Stories of people doing this, with deadly results, abound. In November 2019, a New Jersey woman was found guilty of recklessly causing the death of Yuwen Wang, thirty-nine. Three years earlier, in 2016, Alexandra Mansonet, fifty, had rear-ended a car that had stopped at a crosswalk. Wang, who was crossing the street on foot, was hit when the stopped car jolted forward. She later died at the hospital from her injuries.

At trial, the prosecution alleged that Mansonet had been texting while driving—a claim she denied. The prosecution alleged that a minute before the crash, Mansonet had viewed a text message from her former sister-in-law asking about dinner plans. Evidence presented at trial also suggested that she had begun typing a response when the crash occurred. Mansonet faces five to ten years in state prison.

were not only fighting raging drug addictions, but they were often fighting each other." When she visited her friends, she longed for their normal routines and noticed that their days did not include overturned furniture or searching for parents' missing teeth in the carpet. When Lewis was older, her mother passed away, and she kept in touch with her father through letters. In one of the letters, he wrote, "You know of all the hell that me and Starr went [thru], and the hell we put you kids [thru] was all about the drugs we were addicted to. That was the cause of all the fights, that and not being faithful to each other."[40]

Drugs and alcohol can lower inhibitions, so people are more likely to commit acts that they stop themselves from doing with a sober mind. A person who harbors anger and suppresses it while sober is more likely to become violent when under the influence of drugs and alcohol. According to the Arrestee Drug Abuse Monitoring Program, statistically sampled across ten sites, 63 to 83 percent of arrestees tested positive for illicit substances when they were arrested.

The Vicious Cycle: Recidivism

Addicts who end up in prison often find themselves trapped in a cycle of crime and substance abuse. Natalie Baker was driving drunk when she caused a car accident that injured two people. She spent four years in the Florida state penitentiary. Baker says she found that the prison system is meant to punish individuals rather than to rehabilitate them. In a 2019 article for Recovery.org, she writes, "Behind bars, rehabilitation is virtually nonexistent. Substance abuse is largely ignored and the root causes of addiction are never addressed."[41]

Many experts argue that the system is stacked against addicts. People who are released sometimes overdose in their first days out of prison. When inmates are released from the Florida state penitentiary, they receive fifty dollars and a bus pass, and they usually have little to no other resources or community support. Addicts who do not receive treatment during their prison sentence usually find their way to the next fix as soon as possible. Baker writes, "One girl I bunked next to actually died on her first day of freedom; she tried shooting up the same amount of heroin she'd been using before her arrest. While locked up, her body had weaned itself off of the powerful opiate drug; her mind, however, had not."[42] Sadly, this woman's experience is not unique. A study by the Justice Policy Institute found that 95 percent of drug-addicted inmates use again once they are released, and 60 to 80 percent of them commit new crimes.

"Behind bars, rehabilitation is virtually non-existent. Substance abuse is largely ignored and the root causes of addiction are never addressed."[41]

—Natalie Baker, a former inmate in the Florida state penitentiary

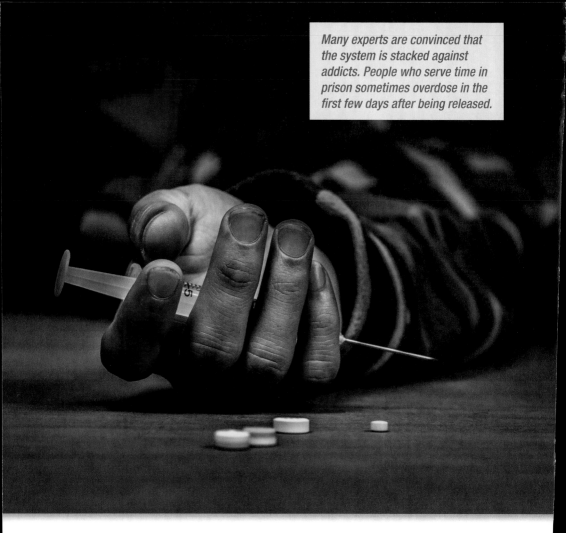

Recidivism rates, or the percentage at which prisoners commit a new crime after they are released from prison, are high across the prison population. There is a direct correlation between addiction and the likelihood to commit a new crime. For this reason, many inmate advocates and policy analysts argue that more needs to be done to address addiction in prisons.

Treating Addicted Inmates

In 2019, the Federal Bureau of Prisons (BOP) offered its substance abuse rehabilitation program, the Residential Drug Abuse Program (RDAP), in seventy-three locations across the United States. Federal prisoners with nonviolent convictions are eligible for the five-hundred-hour treatment program. They further can receive up to a year off their sentence and spend their last six months in a halfway house or on home confinement. In 2018, about 15,600 prisoners participated. The program lasts nine to twelve months, during which time inmates live apart from the general prison population and participate in substance abuse treatment programming as well as work, school, and/or vocational activities. According to the BOP, "Research findings demonstrated that RDAP participants are significantly less likely to recidivate and less likely to relapse to drug use than non-participants. The studies also suggest that the Bureau's RDAPs make a significant difference in the lives of offenders following their release from custody and return to the community."[43]

Many policy analysts suggest that programs like RDAP need to be more widespread and accessible to addicts in the prison system. In the interest of addressing addiction and reducing recidivism, prisoner advocates argue that measures need to be taken to facilitate successful outcomes for released prisoners. Specifically, in its *Behind Bars: Substance Abuse and America's Prison Population* report, the National Center on Addiction and Substance Abuse recommends that prisons and jails do the following:

- Use trained health care professionals for inmate assessment and treatment.
- Provide aftercare plans for released inmates to continue treatment services.
- Require that addiction treatment for inmates be medically managed.
- Expand the use of rehabilitation alternatives to jail and prison.
- Require accreditation for inmates' treatment programs and providers.

Some critics of treatment programs for inmates suggest that the costs are prohibitive. The National Institute on Drug Abuse, however, argues that rehabilitation more than pays for itself with other cost savings. "Drug abuse treatment is cost effective in reducing drug use and bringing about related savings in health care. Treatment also consistently has been shown to reduce the costs associated with lost productivity, crime, and incarceration across various settings and populations."[44]

The fate of the untreated addict is bleak. The destination is often prison or death, and the journey is marred with broken hearts, suffering, and usually crime. Addicts commit crimes to get their next high or because their inhibitions are lowered, and they become violent while under the influence of addictive substances. Many end up in prison or jail, where there is little else than time to prevent them from attaining their next high. When they find it once again—and if they survive—they are more likely to commit their next crime in the process or afterward, and the cycle continues. Treating addiction in prison might be a productive way to help break that cycle.

Chapter Five

Recovery

Recovering addicts face many challenges in the quest to break their addictions. Whether a person is addicted to cell phones or e-cigarettes, stress triggers use. When addicts try to break their habit, they need to find new ways to cope with life's ups and downs during what is often one of the most stressful times in their lives. They also need to completely alter their daily schedules and routines. People addicted to video games spend the majority of their waking hours gaming. When they recover, they need to fill that time and find other hobbies. An anonymous online gaming addict relapsed quite a few times because he did not fill the time void left from not gaming. In his addiction story posted on Game Quitters in 2018, he explained, "I played no games at all, but I also did not replace them with anything healthy or make new friends. I just sat and did nothing, but watch TV."[45]

Addicts also need to repair relationships that might have been harmed because of their addiction and avoid people who are likely to make them relapse. In some cases, addicts have isolated themselves and need to recover without the immediate help of the friends and family they have betrayed along the way.

The battle for recovery is uphill, but it is not hopeless. According to a recent report by the US surgeon general on addiction, only one in ten people who need treatment

> "I played no games at all, but I also did not replace them with anything healthy or make new friends. I just sat and did nothing, but watch TV."[45]
>
> —An anonymous recovering online gaming addict

for addiction receive it. In the case of substance addiction, the relapse rate, which is the percentage of patients who use a substance after being treated, is 40 to 60 percent, according to the National Institute on Drug Abuse. Research shows that community support is paramount in preventing relapses, and recovery programs offer this support for addicts. There are many different addiction recovery programs. One of the most well known is the Alcoholics Anonymous (AA) 12-step program, which has also been adapted to help people with behavioral addictions like gambling and compulsive eating.

AA and the 12-Step Programs

The AA addiction treatment model is based on the view that people are powerless over their addiction and that faith and surrendering to a higher power will help them find a path for living a sober life. Peer support is paramount, and addicts are encouraged to attend meetings often. At the meetings, addicts stand in front of their peers, state their names and addictions, and share their stories of addiction. For these 12-step programs—AA and all of its derivatives—participants are required to have a desire to stop the addictive behavior. Yet even with a desire to change and the help of a 12-step program, recovery is difficult. An addiction does not simply take over a person's brain—it infects all of the person's desires, habits, ability to cope, and social networks. Changing means completely rebooting almost all aspects of the addict's life.

Actor and comedian Russell Brand went through the 12-step recovery for heroin, crack cocaine, and sex addictions. His four-year heroin addiction cost him a job at MTV, a radio show, and relationships with friends and a girlfriend before his manager stepped in to suggest he should attend rehab. Brand subsequently wrote a motivational and comedic book, *Recovery: Freedom from Our Addictions*, based on the 12 steps in order to help others. The reason the 12-step program helped him, he says, is because he was desperate to recover and the program challenged his egocentrism, making him realize that he was not the center of the world.

Under the 12-step model of addiction treatment, addicts are encouraged to attend meetings often. In front of their peers, they introduce themselves and share their personal addiction stories.

Brand writes, "To undertake this process [of recovery], the pursuit of happiness, or contentment or presence or freedom, we have to believe that such a thing is obtainable."[46]

Alternatives to the 12-Step Approach

Some addicts are uncomfortable with the spiritual content of 12-step programs. SMART Recovery, which stands for Self-Management and Recovery Training and like AA offers peer support, is one of the leading alternatives. SMART Recovery uses a methodology called rational emotive behavior therapy to reawaken an addict's sense of reason, generally something that has been smothered in addiction. For example, addicts are asked to do a cost-benefit analysis—meaning they list the advantages and disadvantages of their addiction. The observation that the costs outweigh the benefits, and the extent to which that is the case, is meant to help addicts stop the behaviors that are destroying their lives. Like AA, SMART Recovery has variations for substance as well as behavioral addictions.

Former alcoholic Gentoo (who only uses her first name) credits her 3.5 years of sobriety to SMART Recovery. She drank

Recovering from Food Addiction

Emily is a recovering food addict. Her weight vacillated up and down by about 35 pounds (16 kg) while she was in college. Through her recovery efforts, she has learned that certain foods cause (or trigger) a reaction. "When I begin eating certain foods and ingredients I cannot stop," she says. Then, as happened during this period in college, she obsesses about what she is eating. This in turn leads to depression, hopelessness, desperation, and suicidal feelings.

Emily has had a long recovery road. After college, she tried to recover through a 12-step program, where she had a sponsor and attended regular meetings. For her though, that was not enough. Despite attending the meetings and going to therapy, she was still compulsively eating. Emily decided to put more time and effort into her recovery. In late 2018, she took a leave of absence from her finance job in New York and attended a five-day intensive food addiction program in San Diego, California. The program, SHiFT—Recovery by Acorn, treats food addiction like substance addiction and suggests that, like drugs, the abuse of certain foods changes the brain.

Emily now weighs and measures food according to a meal plan. She remains abstinent from her trigger foods and credits Acorn for her recovery. In a testimonial, she writes, "Thank you, Acorn for helping me realize that none of this is my fault and there is a solution."

Emily S., "How Do I Know If I Am Addicted? Emily's Story," SHiFT—Recovery by Acorn, October 2018. https://foodaddiction.com.

heavily for decades and developed a physical dependence on alcohol. If she went a few hours without drinking, she would shake, sweat, and become anxious. One day, Gentoo fell and hit her head when she was drunk. She suffered a traumatic brain injury from which doctors gave her a fifty-fifty chance of surviving. Gentoo did live, but she had to relearn many basic skills—including how to walk—as a result. The 12-step approach did not appeal to Gentoo; although she went to church, she had a hard time believing that people were completely powerless. SMART

Recovery attracted her because she believed that she had individual power to change her life. In her recovery story, she writes, "I got myself into this, and I wanted concrete, practical, science-based, proven information about how I could get myself out."[47] In the end, Gentoo succeeded. The peer support was particularly appealing for her. She went on to become a facilitator and helps guide group discussions.

SMART Recovery and AA are abstinence-based programs. The expectation is that members will stop using the substance or engaging in the behavior. The Moderation Management (MM) program, on the other hand, describes itself as "a behavioral change program and national support group network for people concerned about their drinking and who desire to make positive lifestyle changes." The MM program encourages people to take personal responsibility for their choices, whether moderation or abstinence. According to the National Institute on Alcohol Abuse and Awareness, there are four times as many problem drinkers as alcoholics across the United States. Problem drinkers use alcohol in a way that has negative consequences but are not yet physically dependent on it. Experts argue that behavioral changes need to occur or these people are likely to become alcoholics. Nine out of ten problem drinkers avoid abstinence-only programs for fear of being labeled an alcoholic or because of the insistence on a lifetime of abstinence. Moderation programs are meant to address problems before a likely impending crisis. The MM program helps people identify the triggers that make them more inclined to drink excessively and provides strategies to help them control their behavior. For example, members are encouraged to plan how much they will drink in advance; delay drinking by participating in certain activities, such as exercise; and reduce the effects of alcohol (by sipping rather than gulping). The MM program suggests that "moderation programs are less costly, shorter in duration, less intensive, and have higher success rates than traditional abstinence-only approaches."[48] Like the other programs, MM suggests that peer support is essential.

Peer Support and Culture in Recovery

Although there is not a one-size-fits-all approach to addiction treatment, the common thread among them is peer support. Research on addiction and multiple treatment programs finds that recovery does not occur in isolation. Peers hold each other accountable, motivate, provide inspiration, and encourage others to cope with cravings. In an interview with the *Los Angeles Times*, Russell Brand explains, "Inevitably, when reason wanes, when the spiritual experience wanes, being part of a community lets you remind one another. Addicts yearn for some sense of connection that makes them feel more healed, more whole, more happy."[49]

Culture is an important component of a peer network and, therefore, of recovery. Addicts have more success if they can find the group that suits their personal beliefs and cultural inclinations. Religion or the belief in a higher power sets recovery programs apart from each other. Atheists as well as many people who frequent religious institutions report feelings of discomfort with the reliance on a higher power in the 12-step programs. People who believe in the role of self-help tend to prefer the other programs. The way people communicate in the group becomes important as well. Some cultures view hugging as a sign of warmth and affection, whereas others feel it crosses boundaries and would prefer not to be touched. Similarly, some cultures value eye contact and active listening, but others view eye contact as a sign of disrespect. Finally, standing before a group and verbalizing the addiction, "I am so-and-so, and I am an alcoholic," might cause overwhelming shame and be prohibitive to one's participation in a traditional 12-step program.

> "Inevitably, when reason wanes, when the spiritual experience wanes, being part of a community lets you remind one another. Addicts yearn for some sense of connection that makes them feel more healed, more whole, more happy."[49]
>
> —Russell Brand, an actor and recovering addict

According to actor Russell Brand, a former heroin addict, peer support is essential for people who are recovering from addiction. Being part of a community, says Brand, can help a person feel more healed, more whole, and happier.

Barriers to Treatment

A significant barrier to treatment is the fact that addicts tend to be in denial or do not want to get help. Taito Kobayashi lives with his parents outside of Tokyo, Japan. Kobayashi plays games on his computer late into the night, sleeps little, and then begins online gaming when he first wakes up in the morning. His parents are concerned about his gaming addiction. In an interview in 2019, his father said, "Online games are the most important

Gender-Specific Treatment Programs

Studies show that men and women often become addicted for different reasons and have different types of addictions. For example, men are more likely than women to use alcohol and marijuana, but women are more likely to report nonmedical use of prescription drugs. Despite the fact that women use certain substances at lower rates than men, their use becomes an addiction at a faster rate. Experts suggest that one of the reasons for this, particularly with alcohol, is the difference in body composition. Women's bodies are composed of less water, more fat tissue, and lower levels of certain enzymes, enabling them to absorb alcohol more quickly. As American Addiction Centers explains, "As a result, women's organs sustain greater exposure to the effects of alcohol, which puts them at a higher risk of developing alcohol dependency more quickly."

The organization argues that because women have different reasons than men for becoming addicts—and because women are more likely than men to be diagnosed with mood and anxiety disorders in addition to their addictions—they face different hurdles in their recovery process. Moreover, some experts suggest that men and women could both benefit from a more tailored, gender-specific approach to their recovery processes.

American Addiction Centers, "Gender Matters When We Talk About Addiction," *The Rehabs Journal* (blog), National Rehabs Directory, November 4, 2019. www.rehabs.com.

thing to him. As parents, we need to consider what we can do to help."[50] Kobayshi recognizes that he has a problem, but he says, "I don't want to quit."[51] Whereas some addicts are in denial, those like Kobayshi recognize they have a problem but do not want to change their behavior.

When addicts decide to get help, treatment can be expensive. In some cases, the barrier to treatment is health insurance. In the United States, the Affordable Care Act (ACA) requires insurance plans to cover addiction treatment, but not all plans are governed by the ACA. By December 2019, only 8.3 million Americans were enrolled in ACA plans. In addition, even when a person does have an ACA-governed plan that covers addiction services, not all treatment centers and health care providers accept ACA insur-

ance. According to the National Survey on Drug Use and Health, in 2018 about one hundred thousand people needed treatment for addiction but could not get it because their insurance plans (some governed by the ACA and others not) either only partially covered it or did not cover it at all.

A person seeking treatment might not have the level of insurance coverage needed. In some cases, an individual might require intensive inpatient treatment for recovery, but his or her insurance only covers a more limited option such as outpatient treatment. Similarly, some insurance plans cover a limited number of days of inpatient treatment, and an addict could be released despite displaying symptoms of imminent relapse.

In some cases, an addict seeking help has the necessary insurance coverage, but demand exceeds supply. In other words, another barrier to treatment is that there are not enough available spots in addiction treatment centers to deal with the number of people who need treatment. It is difficult to get addicts past the first hurdle of denial. When affordability, insurance issues, and vacancies in treatment centers are added to the equation, it is not surprising why so many addicts forgo treatment.

The Permanence of Addiction?

Experts debate whether addicts are forever addicts, even after they have successfully completed treatment. The 12-step programs subscribe to a traditionalist philosophy: once an addict, always an addict. In this view of addiction, addicts are always in recovery—and relapse could be around any corner.

Another view of addiction is that individuals who develop an addiction to one substance or behavior are more prone to other types of addictions. People also debate over this view.

Some experts suggest that it might be possible for a recovering heroin addict, for instance, to enjoy a glass of wine with dinner without a heightened risk of developing an alcohol use disorder. Peter Grinspoon, a Harvard University–trained medical doctor and recovering addict, explains that in his experience, addicts are prone to a particular class of substances or behav-

One theory about addiction is that people who become addicted to one substance or behavior have an elevated risk of developing other addictions. This viewpoint is controversial, however, with many addiction experts rejecting it.

iors. Although he struggled with opioid use, he did not have issues with other substances. A 2014 study published in *JAMA Psychiatry* found that recovering from a substance use disorder made former addicts less, not more, likely to develop new substance addictions. This more fluid idea of addiction suggests that people can change. Those who went through treatment have a new toolbox of coping skills and motivation to handle the lure of other substances. As Grinspoon writes, "Vulnerabilities can improve over time. People aren't static, which is what reminds us to never give up hope when dealing with an addicted loved one, no matter how dire the circumstances appear to be."[52]

"Vulnerabilities can improve over time. People aren't static, which is what reminds us to never give up hope when dealing with an addicted loved one, no matter how dire the circumstances appear to be."[52]

—Peter Grinspoon, a Harvard University–trained medical doctor and recovering addict

Source Notes

Introduction: A Pervasive Problem

1. Quoted in Corey Davis, "Parents Arrested After 11-Month-Old Overdoses on Heroin, Officials Say," ABC Action News, September 26, 2019. https://6abc.com.
2. Melanie Tait, "A Food Addiction Has Defined My Entire Life. And Now It Is Slowly Killing Me," *The Guardian* (Manchester), May 31, 2017. www.theguardian.com.
3. Patrick Carnes, *Out of the Shadows: Understanding Sexual Addiction*. Center City, MN: Hazelden, 2001, p. 27.
4. Quoted in US Department of Health and Human Services, Office of the Surgeon General, *Facing Addiction in America: The Surgeon General's Report on Alcohol, Drugs, and Health*. Washington, DC: US Department of Health and Human Services, 2016. https://addiction.surgeongeneral.gov.

Chapter One: What Is Addiction?

5. Quoted in Physician Health Services, "A Personal Story of Addiction," 2018. www.massmed.org.
6. Jessica Bies, "The Dark Side of March Madness? How to Get Help If You Have a Problem with Gambling," Delaware Online, April 4, 2019. www.delawareonline.com.
7. Michael Pruser, "How I Survived a Gambling Addiction," Dough Roller, December 5, 2019. www.doughroller.net.
8. Randy Kulman, "600,000 Minutes of *Fortnite*? Why Kids Get Hooked," *Screen Play* (blog), *Psychology Today*, March 7, 2019. www.psychologytoday.com.
9. Quoted in CBS News, "Parents Played Video Games as Kids Starved," July 15, 2007. www.cbsnews.com.
10. Quoted in Adam Bisaga, *Overcoming Opioid Addiction*. New York: The Experiment, 2018, p. 52.
11. Judith Grisel, *Never Enough*. New York: Doubleday, 2019, pp. 137–38.

12. Quoted in Abby Goodnough, "A New Drug Scourge: Deaths Involving Meth Are Rising Fast," *New York Times*, December 17, 2019. www.nytimes.com.

13. Quoted in Goodnough, "A New Drug Scourge."

Chapter Two: Why Do People Develop Addictions?

14. J.D. Vance, *Hillbilly Elegy: A Memoir of a Family and Culture in Crisis*. New York: HarperCollins, 2016, p. 116.

15. Quoted in Shatterproof, "Science of Addiction," 2020. www .shatterproof.org.

16. Quoted in Lauren Chval, "Children with Addicted Parents Face Difficulties in Adulthood, Including a Higher Risk of Addiction," *Chicago Tribune*, April 30, 2018. www.chicagotribune.com.

17. Colten Wooten, "My Years in the Florida Shuffle of Drug Addiction," *New Yorker*, October 21, 2019. www.newyorker.com.

18. James Good, "Are Video Games Designed to Be Addictive?," Game Quitters, May 24, 2019. https://gamequitters.com.

19. Quoted in Ethan Gach, "Meet the 19-Year-Old Who Spent over $17,000 on Micro-Transactions," Kotaku, November 30, 2017. www.kotaku.com.au.

20. Quoted in Henry Farrell, "It's No Accident That Facebook Is So Addictive," *Washington Post*, August 6, 2018. www .washingtonpost.com.

Chapter Three: Ruined Lives

21. Quoted in Cathy Free, "A Photo of Her Overdosing with Her Baby in Her Car Went Viral. Three Years Later, She's Sober," *Washington Post*, November 5, 2019. www.washingtonpost .com.

22. Quoted in Free, "A Photo of Her Overdosing with Her Baby in Her Car Went Viral."

23. Quoted in Sarah McCammon, "Knocking on Doors to Get Opioid Overdose Survivors into Treatment," *Morning Edition*, NPR, October 24, 2018. www.npr.org.

24. Quoted in King 5 News, "Third King County Teen Dies of Accidental Fentanyl Overdose," October 4, 2019. www.king5 .com.

25. Quoted in Kim Malcolm and Andy Hurst, "Fentanyl's Death Toll in the Seattle Area," NPR, October 17, 2019. www.kuow.org.
26. Eric McKillen, "The Confessions of a Male, Feminist Sex Addict," Quillette, February 11, 2019. https://quillette.com.
27. McKillen, "The Confessions of a Male, Feminist Sex Addict."
28. Leigh, "My Online Gambling Addiction Ruined My Life," ABC Radio National, September 4, 2017. www.abc.net.au.
29. Leigh, "My Online Gambling Addiction Ruined My Life."
30. Quoted in Suzanne C. Brundage and Carole Levine, *The Ripple Effect: The Impact of the Opioid Epidemic on Children and Families*. New York: United Hospital Fund, 2019. https://uhfnyc.org.
31. Quoted in Dan Levin, "'They're My Safe Place': Children of Addicted Parents, Raised by Relatives," *New York Times*, December 26, 2019. www.nytimes.com.
32. Quoted in Doree Lewak, "Video Game Addiction Ruined My Life," *New York Post*, June 25, 2018. https://nypost.com.

Chapter Four: Crime and Punishment

33. Joe Shrand, "Addiction Is Not a Crime but Can Lead to Them," *Addiction* (blog), *Psychology Today*, January 3, 2013. www.psychologytoday.com.
34. Quoted in Andy Thompson, "In Too Deep: Gambling Addictions Continue to Fuel Large-Scale Thefts," *Appleton (WI) Post-Crescent*, August 26, 2019. www.postcrescent.com.
35. Quoted in Thompson, "In Too Deep."
36. Quoted in Corky Seimaszko, "Women Addicted to Opioids Turn to Sex Work in West Virginia," NBC News, April 30, 2018. www.nbcnews.com.
37. CJBRecovery, "The Economics of Exploitation: The Addicts of Prostitution," The Fix, January 21, 2019. www.thefix.com.
38. Quoted in Khaleda Rahman, "Florida Pharmacy Worker Stole 1,200 Tablets of Strong Pain Killers by Hiding Them in Her Purse and Bra," *Newsweek*, January 13, 2020. www.newsweek.com.
39. Bureau of Justice Statistics, "Drug Use and Crime." www.bjs.gov.

40. Sosha Lewis, "Life Was Hell: My Childhood Story of Drug Addiction and Domestic Abuse," *Charlotte (NC) Observer*, October 30, 2017. www.charlotteobserver.com.
41. Natalie Baker, "My Experience with Substance Abuse and the Prison System," Recovery.org, December 13, 2019. www.recovery.org.
42. Baker, "My Experience with Substance Abuse and the Prison System."
43. Federal Bureau of Prisons, "Substance Abuse Treatment," 2019. www.bop.gov.
44. National Institute on Drug Abuse, "Is Providing Drug Abuse Treatment to Offenders Worth the Financial Investment?," 2014. www.drugabuse.gov.

Chapter 5: Recovery
45. "I'm Addicted to Gaming and I Need Help," Game Quitters, July 14, 2018. www.gamequitters.com.
46. Russell Brand, *Recovery: Freedom from Our Addictions*. New York: Henry Holt, 2017, p. 10.
47. Gentoo, "Gentoo's Addiction Recovery Story," SMART Recovery, 2019. www.smartrecovery.org.
48. Moderation Management, "What Is Moderation Management?" www.moderation.org.
49. Quoted in Roy Wallack, "Russell Brand on How He Pulled His Life Together After Heroin Addiction," *Los Angeles Times*, October 9, 2018. www.latimes.com.
50. Quoted in Al Jazeera "'I Don't Want to Quit': Treating Gaming Addiction in Japan," September 7, 2019. www.aljazeera.com.
51. Quoted in Al Jazeera "'I Don't Want to Quit.'"
52. Peter Grinspoon, "Does Addiction Last a Lifetime?," *Harvard Health Blog*, Harvard Medical School, October 9, 2018. www.health.harvard.edu.

Organizations and Websites

Alcoholics Anonymous (AA)—www.aa.org

AA is a membership organization for people who want to address their drinking problem. It offers a 12-step program and has support groups all around the world. Its website provides daily reflections on recovery and videos of people discussing their recovery experience and how alcohol affected their lives.

Center on Addiction—www.centeronaddiction.org

The center is a national nonprofit organization that addresses addiction by empowering families, working with health care providers to offer treatment, advocating for public policies and resources, and eliminating the stigma of addiction. Its website provides research, statistics, and information on addiction, prevention, and treatment.

Just Think Twice—www.justthinktwice.gov

The US Drug Enforcement Administration created the Just Think Twice website to provide information about drug use and personal stories of young addicts as well as videos and quizzes. Its drug index provides a description of each drug and its paraphernalia. The website further highlights news articles on a variety of topics related to substance addiction.

National Council on Problem Gambling (NCPG)
www.ncpgambling.org

The NCPG aims to help people and families afflicted with problem gambling. It advocates for policies to reduce the effects of problem gambling, but it remains neutral about whether gambling should be legal. The organization's website offers news articles, general information on problem gambling, and contact information for counselors and treatment facilities.

Shatterproof—www.shatterproof.org

Shatterproof is a nonprofit organization whose leadership consists of doctors, executives, addiction specialists, and people affected by substance use disorders. Its objective is to end the stigma and secrecy of addiction and reverse the addiction crisis in the United States. Its website offers news and statistics about addiction, prevention, and treatment.

SMART Recovery—www.smartrecovery.org

SMART Recovery is a not-for-profit organization that uses scientific methods to treat addictive behaviors. Its website offers articles and essays about addiction, information on where to find local meetings and how to connect to online meetings, and a reading list for addictive behavior self-help books.

Substance Abuse and Mental Health Services Administration (SAMHSA)—www.samhsa.gov

Congress created SAMHSA in 1992 to reduce the impact of substance addiction and mental illness in communities throughout the United States. Its website offers a "Tips for Teens" series of fact sheets on a variety topics related to substance abuse and addiction, as well as media highlights of the organization's activities and research.

Books

John Allen, *Addicted to Gambling*. San Diego: Reference-Point, 2020.

Judith Grisel, *Never Enough: The Neuroscience and Experience of Addiction*. New York: Doubleday, 2019.

Carla Mooney, *Addicted to Social Media*. San Diego: ReferencePoint, 2020.

Jennifer Skancke, *Addicted to Opioids*. San Diego: ReferencePoint, 2020.

Bradley Steffens, *Addicted to Video Games*. San Diego: ReferencePoint, 2020.

Internet Sources

Suzanne C. Brundage and Carole Levine, *The Ripple Effect: The Impact of the Opioid Epidemic on Children and Families*. New York: United Hospital Fund, 2019. https://uhfnyc.org.

Henry Farrell, "It's No Accident That Facebook Is So Addictive," *Washington Post*, August 6, 2018. www.washingtonpost.com.

James Good, "Are Video Games Designed to Be Addictive?," Game Quitters, May 24, 2019. https://gamequitters.com.

Shahram Heshmat, "The Role of Denial in Addiction," *Addiction* (blog), *Psychology Today*, November 13, 2018. www.psychologytoday.com.

Tim Newman, "What's to Know About Gambling Addiction," *Medical News Today*, June 19, 2018. www.medicalnewstoday.com.

Colten Wooten, "My Years in the Florida Shuffle of Drug Addiction," *New Yorker*, October 21, 2019. www.newyorker.com.

Index

Note: Boldface page numbers indicate illustrations.

Picture Credits

About the Author

Stephanie Lundquist-Arora has master's degrees in political science and public administration. She has written several books for teens and children. When not writing, Lundquist-Arora likes traveling with her family, jogging, learning jiu-jitsu, reading, and trying new foods.